all about rabbits
by howard hirschhorn

Distributed in the U.S.A. by T.F.H. Publications, Inc., 211 West Sylvania Avenue, P.O. Box 27, Neptune City, N.J. 07753; in England by T.F.H. (Gt. Britain) Ltd., 13 Nutley Lane, Reigate, Surrey; in Canada to the book store and library trade by Clarke, Irwin & Company, Clarwin House, 791 St. Clair Avenue West, Toronto 10, Ontario; in Canada to the pet trade by Rolf C. Hagen Ltd., 3225 Sartelon Street, Montreal 382, Quebec; in Southeast Asia by Y.W. Ong, 9 Lorong 36 Geylang, Singapore 14; in Australia and the south Pacific by Pet Imports Pty. Ltd., P.O. Box 149, Brookvale 2100, N.S.W., Australia. Published by T.F.H. Publications Inc. Ltd., The British Crown Colony of Hong Kong.

Cover photograph: Subject and color
separations courtesy of Sun Chemical
Corporation. Color separations made on
Magnascan 460 Color Scanner.

ISBN #0-87666-214-9

TABLE OF CONTENTS

WHAT ABOUT RABBITS?

Introduction

Rabbit pets are harmless, friendly, and robust. They breed quite easily and may be kept indoors or outdoors year-round.

Domesticated rabbits lend themselves to calm, quiet captivity. They do not, as a rule, become overly excited. They eat well. The well-nigh impossible task of keeping *wild* rabbits is a real challenge to any pet keeper. Wild rabbits, however, will be discussed in this book along with

Rabbits (called "bunnies" when they are young) make excellent pets (see facing page). They also are excellent for food and fur as exemplified by the white New Zealand shown below. Photo by M. Cummings, American Rabbit Breeders Association judge.

Rabbits make interesting pets, pies and petticoats. This is a family of New Zealand whites which seem very nervous about their future! Photo by Claudia Watkins, Ferguson, Mo.

the domesticated ones because a pet book should cover the eventuality of a pet lover bringing home an occasional wild animal in distress.

The three major kinds of domestic rabbit differ as to size, ear length and fur thickness. There are the large breeds, which are usually kept for meat, which include the New Zealand white and the beverans. The soft-coated breeds, kept for their skins, include the chinchilla and the rex. Show breeds, which are used for striving towards theoretical standards of perfection, include the Dutch rabbit and the Belgium "hare."

Domestic rabbits belonging to these three major groups include the so-called *self-colored* rabbits (black, gray, blue, lilac, Havana brown, white), albinos, Polish, Himalayan, English, Siamese, martin, sable, silver fawn, silver gray, silver brown, Flemish giants and lop-ears.

Originally, rabbits were small burrowers from Central Europe and the Carpathians. Greek writers first mention rabbits about the beginning of the Christian era.

Australia, one of the great commercial rabbit-producing areas of the world, had no rabbits before the nineteenth century. Some years after their introduction, a fire destroyed a rabbitry in 1863 and turned them loose into the countryside, where they prospered and multiplied due to the absence of any natural predators. They soon

An English rabbit known as a Netherland's dwarf and his trophies. Photo by John E. Williams.

learned to do such unrabbitlike things as climbing trees and swimming rivers (or perhaps these qualities were instinctive and had merely lain dormant.)

Frantic fencing measures did not halt their advance, even though the longest fence ran for almost a thousand miles. Bounties were paid—one year they were paid on almost twenty-five million rabbits killed—but all to no avail. Nor were poisons, dynamiting the warrens, traps, ferrets, foxes or dogs of any use in reducing the plague of rabbits.

Siamese satin rabbit. Photo by M. Cummings, American Rabbit Breeders Association judge.

Angora rabbit. Photo by M. Cummings, American Rabbit Breeders Association judge.

Rabbit catching was fun and profitable. Australia consequently provided most of the world supply of rabbit fur and meat. Here's why: a single pair of rabbits gives rise to thirteen million rabbits in about three years.

Finally, a virus disease—myxomatosis—caused by the *Myxoma* virus was imported into Australia. Infectious myxomatosis is a fatal disease of the European wild rabbit, domestic rabbits, angoras, Belgian hares, and Flemish giants. Cottontails and jackrabbits are resistant to the disease. Man and other animal species are not affected. Only rabbits succumbed to this "germ warfare" transmitted by mosquitoes, biting flies and by direct contact. Rabbits succumbed by the thousands. Grass began growing again, sheep fattened from the better grazing, and the rabbit population was made more manageable.

Rabbit Ways

Twilight—dawn and dusk—are a rabbit's preferential feeding time in the wild. It does graze about at other times, though, if it feels completely safe. Fright seizes a rabbit all the more, the further it is from its nest. A rabbit signals danger by thumping and displaying its tail as it flees for its burrow.

Anyone who has tried to hold a fidgety rabbit trying to escape knows how its claws can dig right into hands and arms. Grown rabbits, however, have been known to fight rather than run. The rabbit's prime characteristic, especially as far as popular opinion goes, is its timidity. Alice in Wonderland elicits a violent reaction by barely addressing the White Rabbit:

It was the White Rabbit returning, splendidly dressed, with a pair of white kid gloves in one hand and a large fan in the other; he came trotting along in a great hurry, muttering to himself as he came, "Oh! the Duchess, the Duchess! Oh! won't she be savage if I've kept her waiting?" Alice felt so desperate that she was ready to ask help of anyone; so, when the Rabbit came near her, she began, in a low, timid voice, "If you please, sir —" The Rabbit started violently, dropped the white kid gloves and the fan, and skurried away into the darkness as hard as he could go. (Lewis Carroll)

—

→ (Facing page) An Allen jackrabbit catching its second wind out on the Santa Rita Range Reserve in Arizona. Photo by W.P. Taylor, courtesy of the U.S. Bureau of Sport Fisheries and Wildlife.

Black Dutch rabbit. Photo by M. Cummings, A.R.B.A. judge.

Leonardo da Vinci, in the fifteenth century, wrote that the hare is always afraid, and the leaves which fall from the trees in autumn frighten it, even to the extent of sending it fleeing for its life.

Rabbits give birth to naked, that is, unfurred, young. Since the snowshoe "rabbit," that is, the varying hare, and the cottontail "rabbit" are born furred and well developed, they do not fit the description. To confuse the matter even more, neither jackrabbits nor cottontail rabbits burrow. Our wild "rabbits," thus, appear to be hares.

Rabbits and hares live in marshes and swamps, deserts and forests, on the plains, high up at altitudes of 14,000 feet or more, in climates as cold as − 50°F (below zero, that is) or less, and in places as hot as 140°F. The American desert plateau region, however, is their paradise in North America. This region lies in a north-south axis, extending in a 2,000 mile-long and 800 mile-wide band from the northern part of the United States down to the central part of Mexico.

The Lagomorphs

Both rabbits and hares belong, along with pikas, to the *lagomorphs*. Long ears, long hind legs and a short cotton puff tail characterize rabbits and hares. They

Flemish giant rabbit. Photo by M. Cummings, A.R.B.A. judge.

characteristically hop and leap (but the marsh rabbit may occasionally walk or run in a dog-like manner) and are vegetarians.

Rabbits and hares are not rodents. Rodents have two incisors in the upper jaw, but lagomorphs have four incisors in the upper jaw. Such teeth are made for constant munching. Lagomorphs are herbivorous to the point of being serious agricultural pests when too many are at large.

There are two incisors in each jaw, and two additional, smaller incisors behind the front upper incisors. Enamel coats the front surface only. There are no canine, or eye, teeth. The incisors have a wide pulp cavity and are all well supplied with blood; the tooth continues to grow all during the rabbit's life. See the chapter on health for problems associated with this continuous growth.

A cap of skin folds into the space between the incisors and the molars (there are no canines) to work with the

Rabbit teeth keep growing and growing, and they must be used in order to keep them worn down or there are serious consequences. Photo by Claudia Watkins, Ferguson, Mo.

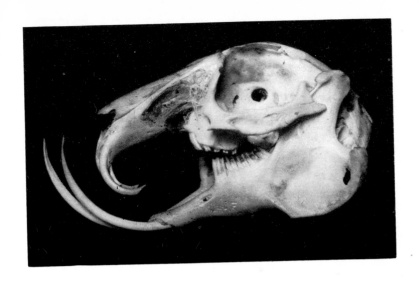

A Colorado coney or pika. Photo courtesy of the American Museum of Natural History.

A
wild
hare.
Photo
by
Claudia
Watkins,
Ferguson,
Missouri.

tongue in manipulating the food about the mouth. The ridges on the molars make them, in effect, self-sharpening.

The jaws grind food between the ridges of enamel on the molars, thus preparing fragments of food to be digested in the long intestinal tract. Microorganisms in the rabbit's gut assist in the decomposition of food.

The chart below compares the rabbit and the hare:

Hare	*Rabbit*
Large size	Small size
Long ears	Short ears
Long legs	Short legs
Fast runner (leaper, that is)	Not good long distance runner
Color changes according to the season	Usually the same color
Nests or builds a "form" but no burrow.	Burrows down into grass-lined dens and warrens. (A warren is a network of burrows and dens.)

As if the confusion of rabbits and hares were not enough, hares have been confused with antelope! The ears of a twenty-three inch prairie hare are longer than the rest of it. Out in their wide-open prairie home—devoid of reference points for comparison—a prairie hare six hundred feet away from an observer has been mistaken for an antelope eighteen hundred feet away!

The following table of comparative sizes and proportions of rabbits and hares will give a quantitative idea of differences. The measurements given are averages made from statistical counts; individuals may vary smaller or larger.

A jackrabbit is really a hare. Photo courtesy of the American Museum of Natural History.

A red satin family scene with the buck, doe and litter. Photo courtesy of Marvin Cummings.

A Belgian hare. Photo courtesy of M. Cummings, American Rabbit Breeders Association judge.

Common Names	Total Length (inches)	Tail (inches)	Hind foot (inches)	Ear (inches)	Weight (pounds)
Pika, Coney, little chief hare, tailless hare, rock rabbit, whistling hare.	7.5	no external tail	—	—	—
Arctic hare	26.5	2.5	6	4.7	10-12
Varying hare, American hare, snowshoe hare, white "rabbit," white hare	19	1.5	5.5	—	3
White-tailed jack "rabbit," prairie hare, plains hare	24	4	6	—	7
White-sided jack "rabbit," antelope jack, Allen's Jack	26	2.5	5.5	6.2	—
Black-tailed jack "rabbit"	28	2.6	—	—	—
Pygmy hare, Idaho hare	11.5	0.6	2.8	2.3	—
Cottontail rabbit	18	2.5	3.4	2.3	—
Swamp rabbit	20.5	2.7	4.2	—	—

Jackrabbits

Jackass-length (almost) ears are what gives this creature its name. And these extra-long ears surely denote their owner's alertness. Extra-long legs, too, characterize the jackrabbit (really, it should be *jackhare*.) It can run ex-

A typical hare (jackrabbit). Photo by Claudia Watkins, Ferguson, Mo.

tremely fast with those legs. A jack was chased two and a half miles by a greyhound, the "slower" dog gaining only seventy-five feet on the hare by the time the hare found a hollow log in which to hide safely.

A jack was seen to clear a seven-foot fence. Another is reported to have leaped a distance of twenty-three feet and four inches.

Champagne d'Argent rabbit. Photo by M. Cummings, A.R.B.A.

Creme d'Argent rabbit. Photo by M. Cummings, A.R.B.A. judge.

The California jackrabbit or black-tailed jackrabbit is a flatfooted broad jumper. It courts in the warm season, usually early spring to midsummer. The female gives birth to a litter of one to five (two to three average) furred, open-eyed young "bunnies" thirty days after mating.

The black-tailed jack is a large hare whose ears are somewhat smaller than the white-sided hare. Its large head sits on a heavy body, supported by very long legs. This desert animal has a very long and thick coat.

Coloration of adults is the same for both sexes, and there is no marked seasonal variation. Coloration is brownish yellow mixed with black above, with the thighs, rump and sides tinged with cinnamon. The tail is pale buff underneath and black above, the black spreading out over the rump.

The doe nurses her young for several days and then scatters them about, possibly as a defensive measure against predators. The young are independent in one month. When grown, the California jack or black-tailed jackrabbit, bounds at forty-five miles per hour.

The white-tailed jackrabbit (alias prairie or plains hare) hits thirty-four miles per hour for fifty yards, and bounds at eighteen to twenty-one miles per hour. This white-tailed jack is a very large hare with long hindlegs and a very conspicuous white, broad and bushy tail, which is rather long for a hare. Its very long ears remind one of those of a mule.

The coloration of the young white-tailed jacks is similar to that of adults, although it is more a uniform slate gray. The male and female adults have identical coloration. In the summer, all of the upper parts, sides of the legs, the throat and the band across the chest are grayish yellow mixed with dark brown. The flanks are lighter gray. The nape of the neck is a smoky white. The undersurfaces of the head and the abdomen are white.

The legs are gray with a rusty tinge. The ear margins are white, and the tips of the ears are black inside and out. In the winter, both sexes are completely white except for the black marks on the tips of the ears.

The black coloration on the tail and rump of this blacktail jackrabbit is not visible in this photo. The black-tipped ears, however, are quite distinct. Photo by C.G. Hansen courtesy of the U.S. Bureau of Sport Fisheries and Wildlife.

Checkered giant rabbit. Photo by M. Cummings, A.R.B.A. judge.

Harlequin rabbit. Photo courtesy of M. Cummings, A.R.B.A. judge.

Antelope jacks (alias Allen's Jackrabbits) do a vertical leap at an easy bound at two and a half to five and a half miles per hour, even hitting thirty to forty miles per hour at times. Varmint hunters pick on jackrabbits because of their eating habits; for example, eight antelope jackrabbits will eat as much as one sheep, and forty-one antelope jackrabbits will eat as much as one cow.

Antelope jacks are quite large hares with very long ears and hindlegs. The head is broad and large, with extremely long ears which are covered with short hairs. A short tail punctuates a large body.

The coloration of the antelopes is identical regardless of sex. There is no marked seasonal variation in coloration. Antelope jacks have been called the most handsome of all the North American hares. Their flanks are mottled white, with gray hind quarters. The antelope jack is yellowish brown mixed with black above, with white and black coloration on the flanks, hips, rump and outside of the legs, creating a salt-and-pepper effect. There is a fulvous band across the chest, but the rest of the under-parts are white. The head is a pale grayish yellow. The

An arctic fox and an arctic hare. Photo by the American Museum of Natural History.

Baird's snowshoe rabbit. Photo courtesy of the American Museum of Natural History.

top of the tail is colored like the back but includes a streak of slate black which spreads over it from the rump; underneath the tail is white. The ears are whitish with a white margin.

The Snowshoe Rabbit

The snowshoe rabbit is also called the varying hare or, sometimes, just plain jackrabbit. It owes its name of *varying* hare to the fact that it changes its color. It is called *snowshoe* rabbit because its big, hair-covered feet work (and make tracks) like snowshoes as the rabbit bounds at four to ten miles per hour in horizontal leaps over the snow. In these leaps it may go as high as ten to twelve feet, hitting thirty miles per hour on a stretch.

The snowshoe rabbit is a good-sized hare, having long ears, long legs and quite a short tail. Its broad head has a blunt nose, large eyes, and quite large ears which are thickly covered with little hairs. The forefeet have five toes and the hindfeet have four toes.

31

An angora rabbit. Photo by M. Cummings, A.R.B.A. judge.

A trio of very young varying hares, or snowshoe rabbits, found near Redvers, Saskatchewan. Photo by Rex Schmidt, courtesy of the U.S. Bureau of Sport Fisheries and Wildlife.

These nervous and timid snowshoe rabbits are colored identically regardless of sex. In the summer they are a cinnamon red above which reaches its darkest shade along the back. Underneath they are white. The ears are tipped with black towards the back, and this black spreads down toward the margin. The front edge of the ear, however, is white. The tail is sooty brown above and grayish below. The throat is a buff brown except the outer part of the chin. In the winter, the snowshoe rabbit is white except the tips of the ear which remain black, the narrow middle band of the ear hair being brownish red. Young snowshoes are grayer than adults but generally about the same otherwise.

A varying hare. Photo courtesy of the American Museum of Natural History.

The snowshoe rabbit courts in the March to August season. At this time, males may fight each other with their teeth. The female gives birth to a litter of one to six furred and open-eyed young fawns, thirty to forty days after mating. The young respond to sound four hours after birth, run on the first day, hop on the third day, raise their ears on the fifth day and nibble hay on the eleventh day. They wean in thirty-five days and are ready to breed in one year.

The Cottontail Rabbit

If very young cottontail rabbits are found wandering about their shallow grass-covered nests, and you cannot possibly resist the temptation to "take care" of them, it may turn out to be a difficult job for you.

Avoid a sudden noise around wild cottontails. They are so excitable just after capture that, if they do not collapse or die of fright when startled, they might frantically try to escape, battering themselves against anything around them. Keep dogs far away from your captive cottontails.

Cottontails are nocturnal animals. They mate year round in the north and for about seven months a year in the south. A litter of one to eight (average of four to seven) young are born after mating. The young leave the nest in twelve days and are fully grown in five months. The parents may mate again before the litter is one day old.

Cottontails can conceal themselves so well that a cottontail doe once was able to raise a litter of fawns in a shallow depression—lined with her own fur—in the lawn of Smithsonian Institute, Washington, D.C., about forty feet from the museum itself and a highway.

A Colorado mountain cottontail. Courtesy of the American Museum of Natural History.

Cottontails are medium-sized rabbits with short tails. The tail has a clear white underside and it is carried over the back of the rabbit so that the white shows. The cottontail's head is rather large, with large eyes and broad, good-sized ears. The legs are rather long, but the hindlegs are not much longer than the forelegs.

Both sexes of adult cottontails have identical coats which vary somewhat, but not too much, with the season. The coat is buff gray mixed and lined with black above. The legs are rufous. A brownish buff band crosses the chest. A broad black edge outlines the ears and tips them. The nape of the neck is rust colored. Each eye is surrounded by a white area. The underparts of the cottontail are white-gray. The tail is brown underneath and white above. Younger cottontails are similar to the adults but do not have the deep black and rufous coloration. Many color differences in the coat are evident in animals which live in different regions.

Swamp Rabbit

This rather good-sized rabbit lives in swampy woods and bogs. It is the most water-loving of rabbits and takes to swimming to escape and to find food. Neither the ears nor the hindlegs are conspicuously long. In fact, the ears are rather short for a rabbit. The tail, also, is very short. The incisors are rather large.

Adults of both sexes have identical coats, showing slight seasonal variation. The color is brown-ochre above, lined with black. The flanks are paler and have less black. The breast is yellowish brown. The chin and the abdomen are white. The tail is reddish brown above and white below. There is a black spot on the forehead. Feet are chestnut brown. There is a dark brown border to the ears with white in front and fulvous behind. A black patch sometimes appears on the cheeks. The neck is reddish brown.

A Wyoming cottontail rabbit. Photo by the American Museum of Natural History.

The smallest of rabbits is the pygmy rabbit, which has been heard to bark while sitting at the entrance to its burrow. This photo by O.J. White of the U.S.B.S.F. & W. was taken in Nevada.

The Pygmy Hare

This most diminutive of North American hares travels close to the ground, and does not leap as most other hares do. It has a very short tail and short ears.

Adults of both sexes are identical in coloration. Variation occurs according to season. In the winter, the long, soft coat of the pygmy hare is drab gray above, somewhat colored with blackish hair. The ears are pale buff inside, and buff-ochre mixed with black-tipped and gray-tipped hairs outside. The ears have black margins to the front. Feet and neck are buff-ochre. Breast is buff-gray. Abdomen is white along the midline. Summer coat is darker than the winter coat, with gray, buff and black above. Coloration of young pygmy hares is like the adults' summer coat.

Prairie hare, female, above. Below, a wood hare and nest. Photos A.M.N.H.

Townsend's hares. Courtesy of the American Museum of Natural History.

Cape jumping hare, also known as springhaar, from South Africa. Photo courtesy of the American Museum of Natural History.

The Domestic Rabbit

This is general information, of course, because the domestic rabbit comes in many varieties. These very promiscous animals have a respiration rate of four hundred and sixty to eight hundred and fifty breaths per minute, a heart rate of two hundred and five (a range of one hundred and twenty-three to three hundred and four) beats per minute, and a lifespan of five to six years, with a maximum recorded age up to thirteen years. One to thirteen young (average of three to nine) are born blind, naked, and closed-earred in thirty to thirty-five days after mating. The eyes of the young open on the eleventh day, and the ears open on the twelfth day. They run on the tenth day and are independent on the thirtieth day. They mate all year round starting at an age of five and one-half to eight and one-half months. If we consider the domestic rabbit by size we can say that the small female (1,500 to 2,000 grams) is ready to breed at six months, has a thirty-day pregnancy, gives birth to a litter of six to eight young which wean at six weeks of age. The young will weigh 1,000 grams at that time. A large domestic rabbit (2,500 to 3,000 grams) is ready to mate at nine months of age, has a thirty-two day pregnancy, gives birth to a litter of six to eight young which wean in eight weeks, and which weigh about 1,500 grams each.

A white rabbit from Douglastown, Long Island, USA. A.M.N.H. photo.

From Asia and western North America comes the pika or coney, *Ochotona saxatilis*. A.M.N.H. photo.

The Pika

The pika might be mistaken for a tiny, brown rabbit —but a rather sluggish one. It is really a lagomorph relative of rabbits and hares, and is also called the coney, the little chief hare or the crying hare (because it does!). Observers have reported that pikas are ventriloquists because it is quite difficult to locate them by their guinea pig-like cries. The pika lives at the greatest altitude (15,900 feet high) of any mammal, but does not hibernate despite its range being high up in the rocky crags of mountain chains (the Rocky Mountains, the Himalayas, etc.). The altitude of its lowest range has been reported as at least 8,600 feet. It gathers hay in the sun, actually amassing little haystacks of winter fodder during its working day. Pika haystacks may be as much as a bushel of dry plant material apiece. In winter, sheepherders in Mongolia take their herds to graze on the haystores piled up at large pika colonies.

Pikas have been fed dandelions, grass, cedar twigs, timothy, clover, alfalfa hay, celery, lettuce, whole and rolled oats, cabbage, carrots, apples, raw potatoes, oatmeal, bread, "Wheaties," and rabbit pellets.

Pikas have been reported to live one year in captivity. These animals cannot tolerate heat above about 96°F.

These diminutive rabbit-like lagomorphs have conspicuous whiskers and broad ears on a rather large and broad head. The thick-set body has no visible external tail. There are five toes on the forefeet and four toes on the hindfeet. The soles of the pikas feet are hairy, giving them better traction on the slippery rocks on which they live.

Adults of both sexes have identically colored coats, with some seasonal variation. Head and shoulders are brownish yellow and the remainder of the upper parts are grayish black. The flanks are brownish yellow. The underparts of the pika are smoky gray, with brown tinges on the chest and abdomen. There is a white border to the ears. The feet are white with brown soles. Young pikas are somewhat grayer than the adults.

This Nubian in a show hutch was just judged Best Dutch Buck, Best Black Dutch and Best Black Dutch Buck. Photo by Claudia Watkins, Ferguson, Mo.

An ideal setup for raising a few pet rabbits in your backyard. Photo by Louise Boyle.

RABBIT HOUSING

A rabbit hutch can be simple or tiered. Folding units and moveable pens are available, or you can build a free-range enclosure.

Place a dry compartment, filled with clean straw, in one corner of the cage. A frightened rabbit will feel more secure having such a corner to run into.

An outdoor pen has advantage in that it helps to reduce the number of rabbit fights . . . and rabbits do fight among themselves. The wire enclosure around an outdoor pen has to be sunk several feet into the ground to prevent the rabbit from burrowing underneath. Some owners plant a shade bush inside the pen (but if its leaves and bark are palatable, it will be eaten!).

An apartment house for rabbits with different tiers for different sexes and/or breeds. Photo by Claudia Watkins, Ferguson, Mo.

The climate determines the kind of housing, in most cases, required for rabbits. Build outdoor housing on nearly level and well drained soil. Provide for some shade over part of the hutch. Allow for ample ventilation and light when constructing. Hutches should be, in general, two and a half feet deep and four feet long. Provide the larger breeds with hutches six feet long. Hutch bottoms can be made of half-inch hardware cloth for the smaller breeds, and five-eighths inch thickness hardwood for medium and heavier rabbits. Wooden slats make good hutch bottoms for the heavier breeds of rabbits. In the north, hutch sides and back should be closed enough to stop the wind from tearing through. In warmer areas, the roof is all that is required.

Hutches can be as simple or as complex as the builder makes them. They may be equipped with food hoppers to hold pellets, water bottles, nest boxes, and racks for dry grasses and hay. Racks and hoppers should be of such construction that the rabbits are not able to contaminate them with their droppings.

If water bottles are not used, flat bottom ceramic crocks are always useful; choose a size that holds about a day's supply of water.

Michael's Rabbit Ranch where cavies (guinea pigs) and rabbits are raised out-of-doors all year round.

The hutch should be constructed in such a way that all of these built-in items can be removed for cleaning and disinfection between litters. The nest box, for example, should be easily removable.

The nest box is worthy of special comment in that it should be sufficiently large to prevent crowding when filled with tiny rabbits, but should be cozy enough to keep these small animals warm as they huddle together.

Wood shavings, straw, or even strips of newspaper make adequate bedding. All bedding should be removed at least once a week and the hutch cleaned well.

The Basle Zoo maintains its European hares in duplexes of large box cages. Every several days, the hares are gently coaxed to change from one to the other of each pair of cages; this permits the unused cage of the duplex to be cleaned without upsetting the animals and causing them to "take off like a scared rabbit." Their initial reaction to fright is to flee, sometimes so strenuously that they either hurt themselves badly on the sides of the cage, or else they *do* escape.

Recommendations for cage size and space allotment according to poundage of each rabbit and to whether rabbits are in groups, alone or are nursing, have been drawn up by various authorities as follows:

Weight	Group of rabbits	Adult individual	Females (nursing)
3-5 lbs.	144 sq. in.	180 sq. in.	576 sq. in.
6-8 lbs.	288 sq. in.	360 sq in.	720 sq. in.
9 lbs. or more	432 sq. in.	———	———
9-11 lbs.	———	540 sq in.	864 sq. in.
12 lbs. or more	———	720 sq. in.	1080 sq. in.

For the professional, this is rather old fashioned, but it served well for many years as a typical angora rabbitry. Fresh air, lots of space and protection against predators, including humans, is a necessity. Photo by Claudia Watkins, Ferguson, Mo.

SHIPMENT OF RABBITS

Before shipping your rabbit, have it in good, well fed condition. Place foods which have a high water content in the shipping container: potatoes, carrots, apples, or lettuce.

Use wood shavings or straw as litter in the shipping containers. Arrange for the fastest carrier, and avoid overcrowding of animals if you ship them in periods of hot weather.

Feeding a pet rabbit a carrot is fun. Rabbits' diets are best met with rabbit pellets which contain all their nutritional requirements. Photo by Claudia Watkins, Ferguson, Mo.

FEEDING

Balanced diet rabbit pellets are available at pet or feed dealers. These pellets can be placed in self-feed hoppers for making them conveniently available to your pet. Good quality, commercially prepared diets for general feeding purposes, as well as special diets for breeding animals, are available. If you buy commercially prepared rations, do not keep them too long before use. Nutritional quality of stored, dried foods drops off with time. Prepared foods, ideally, should be used within four to six weeks after manufacture or compounding.

You should be aware that certain additives (such as estrogen agents) in prepared foods could affect breeding behavior and results.

Once a daily ration has been decided upon, stick to it, at least for awhile. Abrupt changes may disturb your pets. Enteritis and diarrhea may occur in new arrivals because of such sudden dietary changes. Gradually make changes, if any are to be made, in the diet of new arrivals, that is, if you know what they were receiving before you obtained them to begin with. Do not overfeed newly arrived animals.

Theoretical nutritional requirements, in percentages, for growing and adult rabbits, and for pregnant and nursing does are as follows:

Constituent	Growing and Adult Rabbits	Pregnant and Nursing Does
Ash or minerals	5-6.5%	4.5-6%
Fats	2-3.5%	3-5.5%
Fiber	20-27%	14-20%
Nitrogen-free extract	43-47%	44-50%
Proteins	12-15%	14-20%

Here is a typical ration for growing and adult rabbits: four parts by weight of whole grains (oats, wheat, barley,

This is certainly a tame rabbit. . . its eating out of the hand of its owner! Rabbit pellets would be safer; they don't contain insect sprays which probably contaminate this lettuce! Photo by Claudia Watkins, Ferguson, Mo.

soft corn, rye, or buckwheat) plus one part protein supplement in pellet form usually plus all the best quality hay (alfalfa, sweet clover, clover, cowpea, vetch, lespedeza) the rabbits will eat, plus a little green succulent food. Double the quantity of protein supplement for nursing does. Place salt blocks which contain trace minerals in the hutch. When rabbits are fed dry food, provide large amounts of water. Feed your rabbits on a regular basis. In warm weather, rabbits eat more at night than during the day.

Demand (or gravity-feed) water bottles, not troughs or pans, are the best way of providing a fresh, clean source of drinking water. Open containers of water get stepped in, overturned, excreted in, and can become an unsightly (if not downright unhygienic) mess.

A gravity-feed water bottle delivers water due to the force of gravity to a perforated cone or drinking tube attached to the neck of the bottle. The animal sucks or licks water from the opening in the cone or tube; air bubbles enter the bottle, replacing the water being drunk. No air enters and no water drops out when the animal does not lick or suck the opening. The bottle will leak if there is a defect or incorrect adjustment in the system. Leakage can be caused by the wrong size hole in the cone or tube, a bad fit between tube or cone and stopper, or stopper and bottle, agitation of the bottle (water bottles cannot be used in moving vehicles, etc.). Temperature fluctuations will alternately contract and expand the air in the bottle, driving the water out. Contact between the hole delivering the water with objects (or if the animal brushes against it) may start the bottle emptying (the so-called siphoning effect). Fungus, alga, calcareous deposits, corrosion, food, or bedding might block the delivery tube or opening. Bottles that are two small have to be filled too frequently. Water bottles which are too large may empty themselves by the siphoning effect when they are only half filled.

When an animal drinks from a bottle, however, he will still be able to foul the water with saliva and the organisms in its mouth. And some organisms multiply rather well in ordinary faucet water. When room temperatures are high, such water may harbor more organisms after a while than when you put it in the cage. So change water often.

The taste test: when your rabbit is tame enough to take out on a leash, let it sniff out its favorite food each season. Make notes of exactly what it chooses in the field or along the fences where you walk it, and lay in a supply of that plant or pick it fresh at mealtimes.

Young wild bunnies, particularly cottontails, will probably chomp on clover, alfalfa or other greens you give them. They should not be deprived of milk. Use canned milk, and this may be diluted with water, or straight cow's milk can be given. A spoonful of milk can be taken by some young rabbits; otherwise, try an eyedropper or a baby bottle and nipple.

Any nursing bunnies you find in the wild and bring home usually die. (They will probably die in the wild, too, as soon as a predator catches wind of them.) But, if you insist, try rearing them on cow's milk (at your own body temperature) through a dropper or rubber nipple as for the young rabbits above. Nursing rabbits must be kept warm. In a week or so, when their eyes open and body fur begins to grow, you are past some of the dangers of being a foster parent. The little ones can begin nibbling on fresh clover and bread when they are two weeks old, as well as drink some milk. Commercially manufactured rabbit pellets, raw vegetables, oats or hay will soon be appreciated by them. Fresh, leafy green vegetables contain enough water so that the rabbits will probably not drink any, or very little if at all, water. Fresh, clean water, however, should always be available.

Rabbits will also appreciate crushed oats and bran, wild plants from their natural habitats, roots in season (carrots, etc.), hay, cornmeal, barley, boiled potatoes, vegetables and plants such as dandelions, clover, lettuce, kale, cabbage, and even a little meat or fish.

Feeding proper, clean foods is a prerequisite to a healthy rabbitry. These lovely angora rabbits would rather make a nest in their feed bowl than eat from it! If rabbits are overfed they may easily contaminate their own feed with droppings. Photo by Claudia Watkins, Ferguson, Mo.

Some rabbit keepers feed twice daily, particularly young bunnies, with hay and oats, and at least weekly with leafy greens and roots. And weekly, some rabbit breeders give their rabbits a teaspoon or so of cod-liver oil mixed into cornmeal.

HEALTH

Moulting

The rabbit's first moult, or change of fur, is between its first six to sixteen weeks. Add one-half teaspoon linseed oil daily to your pet rabbit's food while it awaits its new coat. This oil supplements the rabbit's natural oils for assuring a glossy new coat of fur.

Initial Check-up

Watch newly arrived rabbits for nasal discharge (sniffles), diarrhea, ear sores, sore hocks, or any injury. Sneezing and sniffling presage a possibly epidemic disease. If your pet continues to do this and worsens, bring it to a veterinarian.

Domestic rabbits bred in colonies may respond poorly to the rigors of being shipped plus having their diets upset; such rabbits may develop diarrhea, deteriorate in general condition, and perhaps die. See your pet dealer or a veterinarian about treatment.

Apparent Coprophagy or Refection

Your pet rabbit's droppings should be firm and solid. Do not become alarmed if you see it eating its own droppings. Coprophagy is the term applied to the rabbit's apparently eating its own fecal pellets directly from the anus, usually during the night about six hours following its last meal. Only the soft pellets, the ones which have passed through the rabbit's digestive tract only once, are eaten, not the true, final fecal matter. Of several theories, one is that the rabbit's nocturnal burrowing life kept it holed up for long sieges by its enemies, and coprophagy is thought to be a normal mechanism to compensate for this enforced state of inactivity and fasting. This habit has an important nutritional aspect, according to some authorities, in that it provides large quantities of vitamin B complex. The

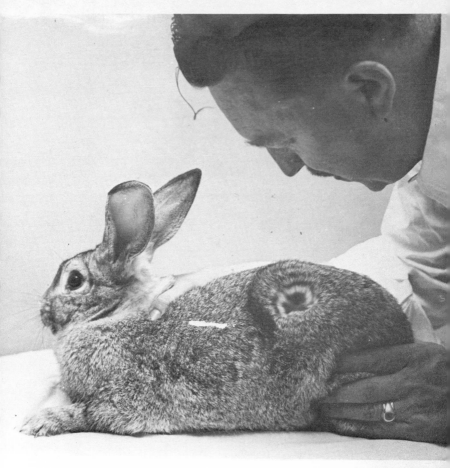

Most rabbits shed their coats three or four times a year. Note the interesting color pattern of the rabbit's undercoat. The veterinarian is blowing into the coat of this rabbit examining him for parasites. Photo by Claudia Watkins; Ferguson, Mo.

rabbit's stomach does not contract very vigorously, thus bulk is needed to push the stomach's contents through the gut. Eating these pellets, then provides bulk, the theory states. Normal nibbling, although often, does not give enough bulk when the rabbit has not eaten for awhile. Only young rabbits on a milk diet do not eat fecal pellets.

Food Hygiene

Illness or even death can be caused by the rabbit's diet, including frosted vegetables or greens, sloppy and dirty food, too much clover, sprouting corn, or unripe roots. Beware of sprayed vegetables. Wash them well, just as you would for human consumption.

Tooth Growth

On first glance it appears that the rabbit has four upper front incisors; but there are only two of them in front. They seem to be four in front because they are grooved longitudinally. (Two other short incisors, not visible, are behind these front teeth.) These two uppers normally meet and grind down the lower incisors. If, however, the lower incisors are not properly met and ground down by the uppers, the lowers *continue to grow* unchecked. The result is disastrous: either the teeth grow up in an arc which fills and obstructs the rabbit's mouth so that it cannot feed, or grows up through the roof of the mouth into the animal's brain, eventually killing it.

Lifespan

Eastern cottontails have been reported to live about five years. The snowshoe rabbit has a recorded lifespan of eight years. The European hare has lived in captivity for eleven years and eleven months.

A Note On Treatment . . . And Not Treating

The treatments suggested here are some of the measures tried by others. Do not consider them sure-cures. Avoid treatment with drugs and medications unless you have expert advice, or clearly understand the instructions which come with the medication. In many instances, rabbit breeders "dispose of" an ill rabbit rather than try to cure it. With pets, of course, one does not wish to take such a drastic step. Consult a veterinarian—a

Doctor of Veterinary Medicine, D.V.M.—when in doubt as to the proper, safe treatment.

Hygienic measures go quite far in preventing disease and curing it by allowing the rabbit's own resistance to help. Nutritional support such as vitamins may help, too. Keep food and water fresh. Keep housing and bedding clean and dry. Remove accumulated droppings. Although animals should be fondled and played with to keep them tame (and they enjoy playing, too!), let them rest quietly awhile if they seem indisposed. You can still "sit by their bedside" and talk with them until they recover, but reduce any rough-house for awhile.

Bloat, Scours, "Diarrhea," Mucoid Enteritis

When this enteritis occurs, most of the rabbits which die are between five and seven weeks old. Mortality then decreases as the rabbits grow older. Affected rabbits are characterized by a rough coat, squinting eyes, lassitude, droopy ears, and lack of appetite. Sick rabbits sit humped over, grinding their teeth. Diarrhea may occur—or even constipation, instead. General hygienic precautions do not stop this disease once it has started. Rabbit feed pellets with antibiotic additives—particularly given during nursing—can be effective in reducing deaths due to enteritis.

Blue Breasts, or Mastitis

The mammary glands of lactating does may become infected by bacteria. The teats become inflamed, swollen and red . . . perhaps turning a blue color later. These does lose their appetite, although they will be thirsty.

A veterinarian sometimes gives penicillin for blue breasts. Good hutch management and cleanliness, as always, goes a long way in preventing infections.

Cannibalism

Do not examine young rabbits too soon after birth, otherwise the doe may kill and devour them.

Coccidiosis

Rabbits may be affected with several forms of this protozoan disease. Young rabbits with liver coccidiosis may lose appetite, have diarrhea and rough coats. Or, they may not show any signs of infection, but can die of it.

Lack of appetite, bloated abdomen (a "pot belly") are signs of the intestinal form. Remove affected rabbits from the group. One of the treatments tried has been sulfaquinoxaline mixed with the food for two weeks; the feed mixture contained 0.1 percent of this drug.

Ear Mites

If your rabbit shakes its head, flops its ears about and paws at them with its hind feet, look for ear mites. Stiff neck and eye muscle spasm, too, are characteristics of infestation with ear mites. Ear mites irritate the ear, leading to the formation of crusts. Dip cotton in a dilute solution of fresh hydrogen peroxide, and swab out the brown crusts. Thoroughly clean and disinfect the hutch. A scabicide can be used (see your pharmacist or veterinarian), mixed with mineral or vegetable oil, swabbing the mixture around the ears as well as down the side of the head and neck, repeating this treatment in six to ten days.

Heat Exhaustion

Pregnant does particularly, but also other rabbits, can succumb to heat in poorly ventilated hutches when the weather is hot and humid.

They lie on their sides, breathing rapidly. To counteract the heat, provide ample water and set a salt block in the hutch. Sprinkle the outside of the hutch with water

Petshops tame their animals, while farms and other outlets sell
wild stock. For pet rabbits visit your petshop. Photo by Claudia
Watkins, Ferguson, Mo.

occasionally when the weather is hot (but keep the inside bedding dry!).

To treat an affected rabbit, immerse the body (not the head!) in a bucket of lukewarm water.

Hutch Burn, Vent Disease, or Urine Burn

Hutch burn affects the vent and external genitals. It is due to flooring in rabbit housing which is wet and soiled. Splashing urine irritates the vent and genital membranes, and this may cause secondary infection from organisms which contaminate the hutch. There may be crusty brown scabs and bloody pus on the affected area. Penicillin ointment helps heal the wounds. Clean and thoroughly dry the hutch flooring.

Mange Mites

Hair loss on nose, chin, head, ear base, and around the eyes occurs when the rabbit is infested with mange mites. A lime sulfur dip may help.

Overdue Birth, Or Dystocia

If the period of pregnancy lasts much beyond thirty-two days, look for signs of distress, such as straining. A veterinarian may give a hormonal injection to hasten delivery.

Ringworm

The fur is thinned out or lost where ringworm (a fungus, not a worm!) occurs, and there are raised, circular, reddened spots topped off with white, flaky crusts. Sprinkle nesting boxes with powdered sulfur before kindling time arrives.

Scabby Nose

This condition is characterized by cracked skin, or

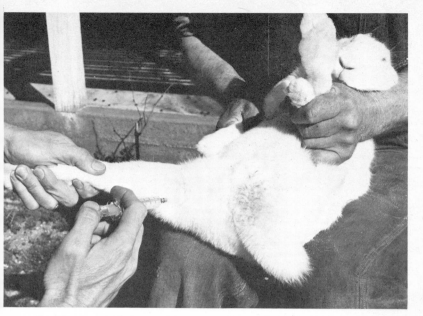

Treating a rabbit for scabby nose with an injection of an antibiotic by a doctor of veterinary medicine. Photo by Claudia Watkins, Ferguson, Mo.

perhaps only chapping, on nose and lips, where brown scales, too, may form when there is secondary infection. Scrupulous hygiene, and treatment of any hutch burn, will help prevent scabby nose.

"Sniffles" And Running At The Nose

There is enough thin or purulent matter from the nose, and sometimes the eyes, for the rabbit's fur to be caked with it on the inside front legs (which the rabbit uses to wipe its nose.)

Sneezing and coughing, too, often accompany the running nose. This disease, also called pasteurellosis, usually occurs in rabbits with low resistance, or at kindling. The organism which causes pasteurellosis can also cause abscesses, perhaps in bucks who have wounds from fighting. Provide proper hygiene and supportive therapy (proper nutrition, clean warm quarters, rest and quiet.)

Sore Hocks

If chafed or bruised hocks become infected, sprinkle with sulfanamide powder. (Excess stomping, one of the rabbit's signal devices, could bruise hocks.) Prevent infections by keeping hutch clean and dry.

Tapeworm

Rabbits can harbor dog and cat tapeworms. Dogs and cats, therefore, should not be allowed near food, water or bedding used for rabbits. (Individual pet rabbits, of course, do not always pick up every disease described in this section, and if "things seem to be going well," one does not always have to suspect the family dog or cat of infecting the family rabbit.)

Weepy Eye, Or Conjunctivitis

Affected rabbits (usually mature bucks and young rabbits) rub their eyes with their front paws, and wipe away the exudate. Use any of the ordinary ophthalmic ointments which contain sulfanamides or antibiotics.

Wet Dewlap

The heavy fold of skin under the neck on some rabbits can become soggy and then inflamed due to the rabbit's dripping drinking water on it. Blowflies may then attack the skin there. Clip the hair from the inflamed area and dust with antiseptic powder. Use a water dish with a smaller opening to avoid splashing, or set the dish on a low shelf.

Wool-Eating

A rabbit may form the habit of pulling wool out from its own back, or the backs of other rabbits. In some cases, wool balls form in the rabbit's stomach and could obstruct passage of food through it.

Rabbits are typical Easter gifts for children. They make excellent pets and are extremely hardy. Photo by Claudia Watkins, Ferguson, Mo.

Terminal Disinfection

Dead rabbits should be promptly removed from a group of rabbits, the other rabbits transferred, and the hutch cleaned and disinfected. This may stop contagious infections from spreading to healthy rabbits, although some may already be infected; hygienic maintenance of the hutch, however, will hold down the disease manifestations or perhaps limit the severity of any outbreak when and if disease finally appears after an incubation period.

Spread Of Disease

The spread of disease among rabbits in a community housing set-up depends upon the following factors:

1. How many animals are already infected?
2. How infective is the disease-causing organism? How soon do adequate numbers get from the first sick animal to the second sick animal, and so on?
3. How potent is the disease-causing organism, and how well does it counter the animal's resistance?
4. How resistant is the animal against a particular disease-causing organism? (Some resistance is natural, some is acquired by previous bouts with the disease, and some comes from prior vaccination or inoculation.)

BREEDING

General

Raising domestic rabbits is not new. The Romans imported rabbits from Spain and kept them in enclosed fields. A painting by Titian (sixteenth century) of a Madonna holding a *white* rabbit reveals to us that rabbits had already been domesticated by then; whiteness is a product of domestication, and will be bred out if the rabbits are allowed to breed freely.

If you choose to breed rabbits, it is advisable to purchase stock with minor defects but from prize-winning lineage rather than mongrels (which, however, can be excellent individual specimens.)

Male rabbits and female rabbits are similar in appearance, although the female rabbit's head is not as round or short as the male's head.

A rabbit's sex can be determined—it can be "sexed" —when it is three days old. It is usually better to wait until weaning time, however, before handling the fawns, otherwise the doe could eat them. Depress the external genitals to expose the mucous membrane. This membrane protrudes as a circle in the male. In the female, it extends into a slit. If you are still in doubt as to which sex is which, however, your rabbits will show you which is which!

The larger the species or strain, the longer it takes to reach sexual maturity. This time ranges from five months to nine months.

Some rabbits breed year around, although the coldest part of the year may cool them down somewhat in their sexual activities.

Buck and doe should be in tiptop shape: alert and active, bright-eyed and glossy-coated. Place doe with the buck for mating. Otherwise, she may fight the buck if he is brought to her, or the buck may not perform on the doe's own grounds.

Rabbits copulate for only a few seconds at any one time.

Shoebox-sized wooden box lined with clean dried grass will be appreciated by the doe. She will add some fur of her own to it. Arrange a doorway close enough to the ground so that the young rabbits, when they are born, can get in and out easily.

The length of pregnancy—usually about thirty-one days—may be increased or decreased by litter size and the doe's weight.

The doe possesses a highly interesting mechanism for controlling the size of her litter. When too few ova are fertilized, these are absorbed right back into her system, saving her the trouble of going through a whole pregnancy just for a few fawns; the doe is then ready again for a more fruitful mating. When, however, the doe is not in the best of condition, or if food is low, then some of the fertilized ova—if too numerous—will be absorbed so that only an "ecologically proper" number of young will be born.

The rabbit's litter will be born in about four to five weeks after mating. The number of fawns in the litter depends upon the doe's health and the food, as was explained above.

Be watchful because bucks may devour the newborn and rough up the doe. Rabbits fight, too.

A rabbit receiving an injection from a veterinarian. Photo by Marvin Cummings.

A litter of Siamese satins in their nest box. The fuzziness is caused by wisps of fur which the doe used to line the nest. Photo by Marvin Cummings.

As the young amble about, mother doe will keep vigilant watch, carrying the wayward ones back home. Although tame does will probably let their owner handle their young, do not handle the young rabbits of recently wild does until they emerge from the nest. (Doe rabbits living in the wild may eat their unfurred and blind young if these are touched by human beings.) Here is a technique for picking up newborn rabbits without upsetting the doe. Delicately pet the doe's abdomen so as to pick up her smell. Give her a morsel of her favorite food—a little distance from the nest—and then, while she is busy munching the carrot or whatever her favorite food is, use your "rabbit-odor" hand to poke into the nest. Quickly count or examine the babies, then replace the nesting material in a way which most nearly approaches the way the doe had it before your intrusion.

Another method to keep the doe from smelling human odor on her young is to rub some Vick's ointment or wax on her nose and front legs.

Here is a baby switch you may carry out if your human smell does not pervade the nest and if the doe is very tame. An overloaded mother doe will not mind your putting some of her numerous litter with another doe who may happen to have a small litter. The two litters should be about the same age and the does should be busily preoccupied away from their nests during the baby switch. (If you fail, one of the does could eat up all the young within her reach!)

Also, the doe could eat her young if she becomes too thirsty.

Feed the rabbit plenty of roots such as carrots and green leafy vegetables, moist ground-up cereals and all the water she wants. One serving of fresh milk daily should be given if the doe drinks it.

Rabbit milk is very rich. It contains one thousand calories per pound. A bottle of cow's milk contains seven hundred and fifty calories and fresh cow's milk only has three hundred and fifty calories per pound.

Care Of The Newborn

Young rabbits leave the nest in about three weeks. Although they now begin to feed themselves, they will also want to take milk from their mother. Two or three weeks of this is normal. Weaning may not occur even for six weeks or so.

The weaning stage is when you must (if you are going to at all) weed out any deformed or otherwise defective young rabbits. Once you have grown attached to them, you will have to live with them . . . at least until their defect proves lethal and nature steps in where you did not tread, killing off the rabbit anyway.

The young rabbits like to stay around familiar surroundings for awhile. Keep their area warm and dry.

Their food—it must be fresh and clean in order to avoid the young rabbits' becoming ill—should consist of carrots or other roots, hay, freshly prepared mash, and, in general, what the doe and buck are eating.

All suckling should cease about seven weeks following birth. Weather and the condition of the rabbit will affect this time somewhat. To encourage the doe to stop giving milk, provide her with a somewhat drier food than usual and do not feed vegetables for a day or so.

Segregate the male rabbits from the female rabbits at about six to eight weeks after mating. Nine to eleven weeks after birth of the young—that is, about when the doe's attention is not so occupied with her fawns—the mother doe and the father buck should be separated unless you wish them to mate again, otherwise they will.

Some Genetic Considerations

The pet owner can control to some extent just what offspring are born. To do this requires some knowledge of genetics—the science of genes and their interactions. Genes, being responsible for the inheritance of characteristics or traits (short hair, pink eyes, agouti-colored coat, etc.), can be *selected for* by the owner. That is, he can pick out parents with the desired characteristics, and then let these rabbits mate. With a little experience, undesirable characteristics can be *bred out* by not letting the animals with those characteristics mate. In general, one can breed rabbits in three ways: random mating, the harem system, and the monogamous pair system.

The random mating system is a free-for-all, or colonial system. This method does not require the keeping of any exact records and requires only that one take the best-looking male (that is, the most virile-looking one) and put him together with some of the best-looking females of the same age group. This method allows large numbers of

animals to be produced and requires hardly any paperwork at all.

Castor rex buck with a doe and litter. Photo by Marvin Cummings,
A.R.B.A.

The harem system is where one "pasha" is placed
together with his bevy of females. The number of females
may range from two to twenty. Some experimentation is
necessary to use this system because not all rabbit and
hare species will mate in such a situation. The harem
method requires very little space and the resulting number

of rabbits born is very great. One should be aware, however, that in the harem system newborn rabbits may be

This type of housing is out-dated and old-fashioned. Photo by M. Cummings.

smothered by their older litter mates or even by the adults.

In the monogamous pair system one encourages nice little "married" pairs, who are kept apart from the others. Individual mating records are possible in this system and this, of course, involves paperwork. The detailed records system is only one disadvantage of this method. Much space and attention and equipment is needed for raising even a small colony.

One should be aware of the existence of linkage in selecting for certain characteristics. Linkage is the tendency for a group of genes to be inherited together continually from one generation to another. Linkages in rabbits may explain some "peculiar" mannerisms in your pet rabbit. Your pet may be that way because it is its genetic heritage!

An example of linkage would be an albino. Albinism is when pigmentation is lacking, making the coat white and the eyes pink. The eyes look pink because that is the natural coloration of the blood in the capillaries, and this shows up when there is no pigmentation to obscure it. The following genetic glossary lists some conditions which may occur in certain combinations with one another:

Albinism—the color of the coat may vary from chinchilla color to complete white

Angora hair—the length of the hair fibers is increased

Brachydactyly—abnormality of the toes

Brown—the color of the coat is brown

Dutch pattern—the coat has a white belt on a colored background

Dwarf—a small rabbit which usually dies after birth

English pattern—colored spots on a white background

Extension—extension of the dark pigment

Furless—the fur is restricted to the extremities

Non-agouti—the color coat is black

Rex—a short plushy coat

Selection of breeding stock depends upon the purposes of the breeders. Wool breeds are the English and French angora. Meat breeds are the white New Zealand, red New Zealand, Californian, Flemish giant and checkered giant. White rabbits (New Zealand, Californian, etc.) are popular because they produce white pelts as well as meat.

Genes are transmitted. Yet, to an extent (sometimes more and sometimes less), definite characteristics are elicited by environment. That is, genes may provide a potential (for something good *or* something bad) only; the forces around the rabbit may bring it to the fore.

Temperature, for example, affects the expression of some genes. The Himalayan fur pattern in domestic rabbits consists of a white coat with black extremities (nose, ears, tail, legs). The Himalayan gene controls the production of black pigment in the fur where the skin is exposed to temperature below approximately 92°F.; and it is easy to see how these extremities get colder than the body proper . . . just as your nose, toes, and fingertips feel the nip of cold weather before the rest of the body does.

To corroborate this is not difficult. If the white hair is plucked from a small spot on the back of a Himalayan rabbit, and ice put on that spot, the skin temperature drops there, and black—not white—hair grows out to replace the plucked hair. The rabbit then has a black spot on its back. This spot gradually reverts back to white as hair grows (assuming that the rabbit is kept at normal temperature) and replaces the black.

If, on the other hand, the black hair is plucked from the rabbit's extremities, say from one of its paws, and the denuded area covered with a heating pad, then white hair will grow there.

Mating To Weaning Time And Other Vital Statistics

The figures below are averages for several species *in general*, and are meant only to provide a notion of relative time. Each species shows quite a range of variation. See under individual species for closer approximation.

These modern wire cages for rabbits are clean and well lit. They are constructed of mesh small enough to keep the rabbit's feet from poking through, yet large enough to allow the debris to fall through to the absorbent material underneath. Photo by Marvin Cummings.

This is a typical, modern carrying cage large enough for three rabbits. Photo by Marvin Cummings.

	Mating to Birth	*Birth to Weaning*
Mice	20 days	18 days
Rats	21 days	21 days
Rabbits	31 days	42 days

More specifically, the following table provides a relative notion of just where rabbits and their vital statistics stand in comparison with other small animals and *their* vital statistics:

	Mice	*Rats*	*Rabbits*
Gestation (days)	17-21	19-22	28-31
Estrous cycle (days)	4-5	4.5	Rabbits are induced ovulators
Litter size (individuals)	12	12-14	5-12
Age when breeding stops (months)	9	9	24
Number of babies produced by each female in 100 days	21-35	21-28	30

RABBIT HANDLING

Never use your pet's ears as a handle with which to lift it. Place one hand under its rump or abdomen and steady it, perhaps gently holding the ears with the other hand, or grasp the loose skin over the withers, and you will have a good hold of it. When the rabbit is tame, pick it up as you would a cat or dog.

A New Zealand white doe and her fryer production for 12 months. USDA-BAI 82704B.

The following passage by John Burroughs, an American naturalist, tells us something about the wild rabbit's propensity for taming, as well as warns us to provide our pet rabbits with protection from predators:

Winter, like poverty, makes us acquainted with strange bedfellows. For my part, my nearest approach to a strange bedfellow is the little gray rabbit that has taken up her abode under my study floor. As she spends the day here and is out larking at night, she is not much of a bedfellow, after all. It is probably that I disturb her slumbers more than she does mine. I think she is some support to me under there—a silent, wide-eyed witness and backer; a type of the gentle and harmless in savage nature. . . . I think I can feel her goodwill through the floor, and I hope she can mine. When I have a happy thought, I imagine her ears twitch, especially when I think of the sweet apple I will place by her doorway at night. I wonder if that fox chanced to catch a glimpse of her the other night when he stealthily leaped over the fence near by and walked along between the study and the house?

Two ways of holding a rabbit. An owner will soon feel his or her own way of gently restraining a jumpy rabbit. After a little petting and hand-feeding, however, the rabbit will probably not want to jump away but will follow behind his master. NEVER LIFT A RABBIT BY ITS SENSITIVE EARS! Photos by Marvin Apfelbaum.

RABBIT CLUBS, STANDARDS AND SHOWS

The American Rabbit Breeders Association is the parent organization of all the rabbit clubs in the U.S.A. It licenses all rabbit judges and registrars, maintains records of all registered rabbits, and provides many services to all rabbit breeders. The American Rabbit Breeders Association holds annual conventions and shows.

There are national specialty clubs as well as state and local clubs. All of these groups are chartered by the American Rabbit Breeders Association. National specialty clubs sponsor and promote only one breed. State and local clubs are made up of rabbit breeders and are primarily engaged in promoting the raising of rabbits and in helping beginners on a local, personal level. American Rabbit Breeders Association (ARBA) now has about 15,000 members nationwide.

Each breed of rabbit has a feature that sets it off from other rabbits. Each breed is judged in shows on its own merits and by its own standard—a set of theoretical requirements of perfection. Judging is by comparison with other, similar rabbits, and by a point system.

Each breed of rabbit has a total allocation of one hundred points, these points being divided according to the prime feature of the breed being judged. A New Zealand, for example, primarily a meat breed, has fifty-five points allotted to body type or conformation. An English lop-ear, on the other hand, is primarily a fancy breed and has only ten points allotted to body type. The lop's outstanding feature—massive, long, drooping ears—has fifty-five points allotted. (The New Zealand, by comparison, has only two points allotted for ears.)

The Dutch breed is raised and judged mainly for its markings and how they are placed, so, in the Dutch, only thirteen points are allotted to color, whereas in the silver breed, color is quite important, so sixty points are allotted

Black Dutch buck. Photo by Michelin Animal Photography, Rutherford, N.J.

to color in silvers. In summary, what is important in one breed may be insignificant in another.

Judges at rabbit shows first divide the contestants into breeds and then into varieties within a breed. Then the rabbits are further classed according to age and to sex. The judges then eliminate the poorer rabbits until they have the best in each class. From these, the judges select the *Best of Breed*. Eventually, all of the best of breeds are judged against one another and the standards for their respective breeds until the *Best of Show* is selected.

PROFITABLE COMMERCIAL ASPECTS OF RAISING ANIMALS

Medical Research

Rabbits, along with rats and mice, constitute the major percentage of animals used in research; in the U.S.A., for example, mice accounted for about 65% of vertebrates

A Californian breed rabbit. Photo by M. Cummings, A.R.B.A. Judge.

English spot rabbit. Photo by M. Cummings, A.R.B.A. judge.

used in laboratories several years ago, rats about 22%, and rabbits about 1.1%. Laboratories use animals for research into the cause and cure of cancer and tumors, for testing the harmlessness (or dangers!) of food color or flavor additives, and for testing drugs intended for human consumption.

The thalidomide incident—when babies with limb deformities were born to mothers who had taken this drug during pregnancy—inspired a greater testing of new drugs in animals before the release of these drugs for use in human beings. Thalidomide was found to cause much the same teratogenic effect (abnormalities and malformations) in pregnant rabbits as it did in human beings. Rabbits, therefore, are now being used quite extensively for this purpose, although rats are now beginning to contribute, too.

Large numbers of rabbits, rats and mice, as well as other small animals, are used in the bioassay of literally thousands of prophylactic and therapeutic substances before the U.S. government will permit these substances to be released for sale to the public. Universities, research institutes and foundations, cancer research units, hospitals, U.S. Public Health laboratories, and the pharmaceutical industries are the organizations which use these animals for the above purposes.

Rabbits, mice and rats are also used for the laboratory diagnosis of diseases and of pregnancy in human beings. A specimen of some biological substance (blood, urine, pus, etc.) is taken from the human patient and inoculated into the test animal. The animal becomes ill, or shows a characteristic change (not always fatal or harmful to the animal), thus proving the existence of a certain disease organism. Or, as in the case of pregnancy tests, the animal—if the test is positive—may show certain physiological changes in response to its inoculation with urine from a woman who is pregnant.

Rabbits for Fur and Meat

Rabbit fur and meat have become significant items of international trade and economics. Rabbit and hare fur, or coat, varies according to breed and condition of the individual, and the color of the coat is dictated by geography and climate. For example, the Greenland hare in the north has a long, dense wooly coat. The Tehuantepec cottontail in southern Mexico has a thin, short and coarse coat. Coat color also responds to climate. Species which have two annual moults are white in winter and dark in summer. In northern Greenland, however, hares remain white all year long.

The coat consists of three sets of hair: closest to the body is a dense underfur made up of fine short hairs; next there are longer and thinner hairs making up a coarser coat, tips of which just cover and conceal the underfur; and on top is a still longer, coarser, more sparsely distributed set of hair, the tips of which cover the shorter middle coat.

Rabbits are sacrificed for fur when they are about three months old. At that age there is no down, but the rabbit's fine and closely set hair lays randomly enough to give a moiré effect.

Excellent workmanship and tricks of the trade have given some commercial value to rabbit skins and furs. Rabbit fur can be made to imitate many of the more expensive pelts. The rabbit itself can even have the aspect of the animal whose fur it imitates. Chinchilla rabbit and silvers (or argents) simulate chinchillas and silver foxes, respectively. Rabbit fur has more "exciting" names in the trade: Arctic fur, clipped seal, polar seal, lapin.

For the beginning rabbit keeper, plain white rabbits are best. Experienced furriers can dye and work these basic pelts into more valuable furs.

If a rabbit fur of x size is worth x dollars, would a fur of 2x size be worth 2x dollars? Perhaps, if the rabbit's

A black silver rabbit. Photo by M. Cummings, A.R.B.A. judge.

A chinchilla rabbit. Photo by M. Cummings, A.R.B.A. judge.

This angora rabbit can produce enough wool to make two sweaters every year! Photo by Claudia Watkins, Ferguson, Mo.

meat were not being considered. Where a rabbit is reared as large as possible, in order to have as large a pelt as possible, the quality of the meat may drop. The full value of the fur is reached only when the rabbit gets older. Meat from older rabbits, however, is not of maximum value.

Indians and Rabbitskins

Twisted strips of rabbit fur were woven on a loomlike frame into blankets and robes by Indians living in an area extending from the Yucatan peninsula of Mexico all the way northwards, over the great plateau in the U.S.A. and up into Canada.

To make a rabbitskin blanket or robe, the skin is cut into long strips and twisted so as to produce fluffy cords. These furry cords are then woven in a loose fashion until a rectangular blanket or robe is produced.

Indians organized mass community rabbit hunts, sometimes using special cudgels and throwing sticks to capture their dodging prey.

Rabbit and Hare Meat

The following table represents a comparison of rabbit and hare meat with a common poultry item (a roasting chicken) and cutlets from a common meat animal (hog).

Food Value of Rabbits and Hares Compared with Chickens and Hogs

Substance per 100 grams of edible portion	Rabbit	Hare	Chicken (roasting)	Hog (cutlet)
Water (grams)	70.4	73	66.9	53.9
Calories (kcal)	159	103	197	341
Protein (grams)	20.4	22.3	19.5	15.2
Carbohydrates (grams)	0	0.2	0	0
Fats (total, grams)	8.0	0.9	12.6	30.6
		(tocopherol)		
Polyunsaturated fats (grams)	1.5	—	—	2.8
Cholesterol (grams)	0.12	0.08	—	0.07
Vitamin A (IU)	30	0	410	0
Vitamin B_1 (mg)	0.04	0.09	0.08	0.8
Vitamin B_2 (mg)	0.18	0.19	0.12	0.19
Vitamin B_6 (mg)	0.6	—	—	0.48
Vitamin C (mg)	0	—	—	0
Nicotinic acid (mg)	12.8	5.0	7.4	4.3
Pantothenic acid (mg)	0.8	—	—	0.40
Sodium (mg)	40	50	—	62
Potassium (mg)	385	400	—	326
Calcium (mg)	18	12	11	10
Magnesium (mg)	—	—	—	19
Manganese (mg)	—	—	—	0.06
Iron (mg)	2.4	3.2	1.5	2.6
Phosphorus (mg)	210	157	191	193
Sulfur (mg)	199	—	—	—
Chlorine (mg)	51	—	—	—

mg = milligram(s)
IU = International Units
— = no information available

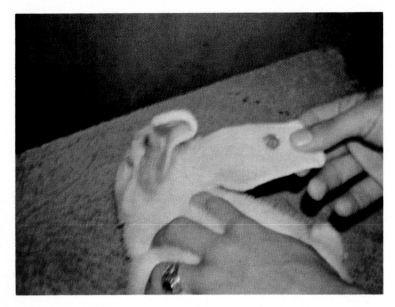

Tattoos on the inside of the ear identify rabbits permanently. Photo by Claudia Watkins.

A white Polish rabbit. Courtesy of M. Cummings, A.R.B.A. judge.

Contentment and beauty. Captivatingly photographed by Mervin F. Roberts.

A standard chinchilla doe. Photo by Claudia Watkins, Ferguson, Mo.

The standard black silver giant on the facing page is shown below compared to a pet white rabbit. Photos by Claudia Watkins.

It will be seen from the foregoing table that rabbits and hares are less in calories than pork and chicken, less in total fats, and higher in proteins. Interesting differences, too, are seen between rabbits and hares. Their biochemical make-up is due to some extent to their diets and ways of life, which, as explained earlier in this book, differentiate these two groups of lagomorphs.

FINAL THOUGHTS ON RABBIT THEORY

An animal built for escaping is what you have in your rabbit. It can burrow although one would not guess that from the construction of its paws. A hare does not burrow but is built quite similarly. Domestic rabbits dig right in after escaping their cages. A theory has it that rabbits learn to burrow as an escape from cats, dogs, foxes and other predators. Rabbits in high mountainous areas without these risks to their life do nest at ground level. And yet, rabbits are born blind and weak, and that is not very much protection for animals out in the open, while hares, which do not burrow, can run shortly after birth. And to top it all off, rabbits have been known to hide out in trees. In short, rabbit owners have an opportunity to observe their pets and perhaps contribute to the yet incomplete store of knowledge of just why rabbits do as they do, and are as they are!

Is it any wonder a million rabbits are sold every year for pets? Photo by Marvin Apfelbaum.